GENDER

First published 2021 by order of the Tate Trustees
by Tate Publishing, a division of Tate Enterprises Ltd,
Millbank, London SW1P 4RG
www.tate.org.uk/publishing

© Tate Enterprises Ltd 2021
Text © Travis Alabanza 2021

Copyright
All images are © the artists unless stated otherwise
© Ajamu X
Reproduced by permission of The Henry Moore Foundation

Photo credits
All images are © Tate Images 2021
Tate Images Sam Day p.45

A catalogue record for this book is available from the British Library
ISBN 978 1 84976 715 6

Distributed in the United States and Canada by ABRAMS, New York

Library of Congress Control Number applied for

Senior Editor: Alice Chasey
Series Editors: Mels Evers and James Finch
Production: Juliette Dupire
Picture Researcher: Roz Hill
Designed by Narrate + Kelly Barrow
Colour reproduction by DL Imaging, London
Printed in Wales by Cambrian Printers

Front cover: Marcus Gheeraerts II, *Portrait of Captain Thomas Lee* 1594 (detail, see p.33)

Measurements of artworks are given in centimetres, height before width, before depth.

GENDER

TRAVIS ALABANZA

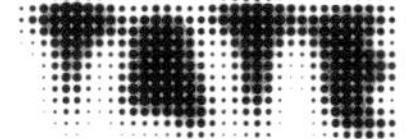

Director's Statement

'Look Again' is a bold new publishing programme from Tate Publishing and Tate Britain. In twelve books, published in three stages, we are providing a platform for some of the most exciting contemporary voices writing today to explore the national collection of British art in their own way, and reconnect art to our lives today. The books have been developed ahead of the rehang of Tate Britain's collection, which will be launched in 2023 and will foreground many of the artworks discussed here. In these first four texts – *Gender* by Travis Alabanza, *Feminism* by Bernardine Evaristo, *Empire* by Afua Hirsch, and *Class* by Nathalie Olah – we are offered unique perspectives on a wide range of artworks across British history, and encouraged to look closely, and to look again.

Alex Farquharson, Director, Tate Britain

It was the American philosopher Judith Butler who said, 'Gender is a performance.' She, as well as the hundreds of drag queens I have met in the underground queer bars of London, reminds us of the acts of drama that go hand-in-hand with our experience of gender: a man spreading his legs on the Tube; a woman showing her biceps in a boiler suit saying, 'We Can Do it!'; or a stiletto heel stepping on a briefcase. It seems wherever gender goes, there follows a performance of what it might be trying to say.

Or is it more accurate to propose that gender forces the subject to appear disingenuous, in order to avoid the pitfall of a performance that feels too obvious to an audience? It is as if gender can never seem effortless, in the same way that you can tell when an actor is focusing too hard on remembering their lines.

I am neither the first nor the last person to start a piece of writing analysing gender with Judith Butler, or that particular phrase. (If this was a student essay on gender I would have just been marked down for lack of originality.) I believe, however, that there is something in the popularity of a phrase. It is hard to mention gender, let alone look closely at it, without discussing the aspect of performance to which it is linked. I cannot begin to think about gender without

"IT IS HARD TO MENTION GENDER, LET ALONE LOOK CLOSELY AT IT, WITHOUT DISCUSSING THE ASPECT OF PERFORMANCE TO WHICH IT IS LINKED."

seeing how absurdly we do things to try and sustain it. We might play with our hair in a certain way, place a hand on a hip, pick a certain drink, paint a wall a specific colour, walk with a certain stride – all to try and ensure that someone sees us in a way that aligns with expectation. We are all in a very long durational performance piece with gender. It is almost as if one cannot exist without the other. If there is no one around to make a show for, would your gender still turn up to take the bow? If there were no genders around to provoke us into performance, would we still feel the need to make a show?

Similarly, I believe art is also wrapped up in performance. I see a piece of art as a still of a performance in motion, a moment of drama, a snapshot, a glimpse into a spectacle – it captures a breath to be immortalised. And, as I am given the task of observing gender in these pieces of art, it feels important to ask you to walk into the performance that surrounds it, and to ignore those trying to abide or resist or confuse or compel us within it. To indulge in the drama that always follows gender. To indulge in the drama that always follows art.

This gallery, being Tate Britain, may not have been asked to be reviewed in this way; it often seems things that are left for a long time often want to be left alone. Some works may never have asked for such a lens to be turned upon them, but equally many of us ask not to be gendered, and yet here we are, gendered, without a choice, every day. Gender is like a fog that cannot lift, or a filter that cannot be removed, even in our choice to ignore it – it will still be there. There are some works that want to meet gender right in the middle of the road, to hit it head on, to put spotlights on it, to place it on podiums for us to celebrate or condemn. Others are asking us to bend it, challenging us to rethink it, insisting on a pause allowing us to see it in another way. Many works may not be thinking about it at all, but it is all I can think about when looking at them. Others still I was surprised to mention here, but after meeting them, staring at them in the gallery, the tale I tell would not make sense without them.

A performance is defined in many ways. It could be the production of an entertainment on stage, the action of carrying out a task or a function, the display of exaggerated gestures to complete a simple task ('Oh, what a performance!'), or the act of presenting something to convey an idea or message to a viewer. Both gender and art are about the performance.

In this book I am going to discover who is really putting on a show, and what they are telling us. As the performer, someone who owns what we are all already doing, it feels like the perfect way to look at this gallery and gender. As the audience, I will try to identify the performance through the way the works make me feel, with the hope that I can find a home or some comfort in two things in which I often feel uncomfortable: the gallery and gender.

And so, without further ado, let the show begin ...

INSIDE THE GALLERY

A play in two parts.

PART 1
(see p.33)

1594: Captain Thomas Lee is standing for a portrait by the artist Marcus Gheeraerts. Gheeraerts has set up his easel in the long grass, and Lee is wearing his finest regalia – a fantasy evocation combining the dress of an Irish soldier and that of a Roman hero, which would maybe now be found in the women's section of Zara. They have been trying to get the right pose for hours.

Gheeraerts: Captain, that is perfect! Yes, hold that pose. Keep the wrist limp and the dress short.

Lee: You think it's too much? I want it to say power!

Gheeraerts: Too much? It's the '90s; there can never be too much! And nothing says regal power like a limp wrist; it's a timeless choice.

Gheeraerts continues to paint, as Lee looks proudly at his limp wrist.

PART 2
(see p.34)

Two Cholmondeley Ladies are lying in bed together. Identically poised. Not touching. Carrying babies in their arms.

Cholmondeley Lady 1: How long do we have to hold our arms like this? The baby is getting heavy…

Cholmondeley Lady 2: For as long as it takes them to capture us in motherhood.

Cholmondeley Lady 1: At least I get to lie next to you…

Cholmondeley Lady 2: What?

Cholmondeley Lady 1: Nothing. I said, at least the bed is comfy!

The Two Cholmondeley Ladies continue to sit in bed and be painted, unaware of the mystery that will be drawn around them.

A NOTE FOR ANY ACTORS WISHING TO PLAY THE MAN

Thank you for agreeing to play THE MAN in this production of MOST THINGS THAT CONTAIN A MAN. *These are just some notes with which to acquaint yourself before you read the script and to familiarise yourself with the role titled THE MAN. All good actors acknowledge that a part cannot be adequately played without research. To simply read the script is to create only two dimensions, when of course we always aim for the third. A third dimension is always found in the research, in the study, in the observation. If you need further references, may I suggest standing boldly in front of* The Death of Major Peirson *(see no.p.35), or the portrait of* Colonel Acland and Lord Sydney *(see no.37), or* The Hopes of The Party, *or Cruikshank's* Manchester Heroes, *or the many other depictions of THE MAN from 1600 to 1800. You will see that to play THE MAN you must also be holding, using, running with, or at arm's reach from a weapon. THE MAN and a weapon are never too far apart. A weapon becomes an extension of THE MAN, almost as if it is impossible to be THE MAN without fighting something. The more you show you can fight, the more successful your performance of THE MAN will be. THE MAN is naturally at his most THE MAN when he is in battle, ideally in battle with other men. In order to win at masculinity you must be shown killing all the other signs of it. If THE MAN is not shown in battle, make sure a gun is still in his hand, or slightly off stage, or in the background, or on a crest, or that he wears a glove which suggests he was just holding one – just in case the viewer might forget that this is THE MAN that battles, that carries weapons, that fights, and is therefore still THE MAN. The idea you must emote the most as THE MAN is that of war. There is no happiness, or sadness, or warmth, or desire, or lust, only fight, war, kill, battle. Before you take on this role, ensure you familiarise yourself with what it feels like to be in battle, with yourself or others or gender, who knows, and ensure that you are only shown in direct relation to your ability to fight. THE MAN is at war with HIMSELF/WAR/OTHER MEN.*

A SCENE CHANGE

Directions for the stage manager of this production of SOMETHING ABOUT GENDER IN THE GALLERY.

As we change scenes, from a note for any actors wishing to play THE MAN to a note for any actors wishing to play THE WOMAN, it seems important to mention that, even within this deliberate set-up, we are already failing. To talk about gender and its expression or possible queerness, within the structures of only men and women, is to miss out on a history and present that always existed. The first violence is the act of gendering, then to decide there are only two is to kill or erase or never archive all those that said they were neither. It feels an impossible task to solve this within one play, so instead we suggest this scene change to bring attention to the limitations of the work. How can we talk about the gender of a gallery, if not all the genders are even present? How can we discuss gender, and its presentation of men and women, if we are not even trusting of an archiver to ask enough questions to ensure they were men and women in the first place? How do we talk about people's genders, if we know too well that how we see someone's gender is often not what they wish they could show? We are taught to observe what we see, but so much of our gender is caught up in the imagination of what we could be.

This feels like an incredibly hard task for the play SOMETHING ABOUT GENDER IN THE GALLERY *to achieve with any success, so may we suggest that during this scene change from THE MAN to THE WOMAN you hold up Brechtian placards explaining the existence of people outside of those categories, about the limitation of categories, about the history of gender non-conforming people throughout time. You may need very large placards. Hold them up as you change scene, so people know what comes in between.*

A NOTE FOR ANY ACTORS WISHING TO PLAY THE WOMAN

Thank you for agreeing to play THE WOMAN in this production of MOST THINGS THAT HAVE US IN THE BACKGROUND. These are just some notes with which to acquaint yourself before you read the script and to familiarise yourself with the role titled THE WOMAN. All good actors acknowledge that a part cannot be adequately played without research. To simply read the script is to create only two dimensions, when of course we always aim for the third. A third dimension is always found in the research, in the study, in the observation. Of course, dimensions are much easier to find in research if you are playing THE MAN, whereas for THE WOMAN you must be skilled in the art of searching for crumbs, an exercise that will be similar to that of searching for dimensions in an archive. If you need the references, may I suggest sitting slightly aloof in the Pre-Raphaelite room, staring into the middle distance slightly to the left, refusing to look straight on. It is important to note that for the role of THE WOMAN you must be white. There is not an explanation for that; just simply from our research of the archive and of what is shown, it seems that is all there is. You will be white, and you will be pale in order to be counted as THE WOMAN. Once you have perfected the whiteness of femininity, if that is not in antithesis, it is important to perfect the expression of longing for something else. You will often be looking aside in longing. Figure out what that longing is for you and capture it. Maybe it is a longing to not be reduced to your appearance, or a longing to have your boss not undermine your aptitude for a task; maybe it is a longing to be seen as a woman who can long for something; maybe it is a longing to be able to be seen in something other than longing – but you must perfect your longing. If you need reference for your longing, put on as many clothes as possible and look at Gretchen (see p.38), The Bride (see p.39), or Symphony in White, No. 2: The Little White Girl (see p.41). *Of course, as with most things in life, we should expect exceptions. If you do not get the part of longing, you may also be cast as 'simply lying down', as modelled in* Ophelia (see p.43). *Do not see this as a bad part. Sometimes, lying down and surrendering to what gender may bring us, solves any pain in the neck from longing for more. If you find whiteness is not something you can obtain, it seems then, as usual, you must become familiar with being in the background of the background. Holding something up perhaps? Maybe a light to shine on someone else, or a flower to make someone else bloom brighter? For you, who knows what gender is, for we cannot get past the barrier of your skin to get there.*

TWO MONOLOGUES FOR THE RULE BREAKERS

A monologue for the part of Maud Allan. The scene is sometime after the 1920s. After the court cases, the conspiracy around her sexuality, the arrests, she is somewhere with her lover and secretary – away from it all.

Maud *[while looking at a portrait of herself and speaking to Verna Aldrich]*: I wonder if one day they will hang this in galleries, Verna? In the big fancy ones, the ones that represent everything of timelessness, of adoration, of obtaining success. And I will turn around and say: 'Is that not everything you said I was not?' I wonder if in the plaque underneath, explaining who I was and what I did, they will simply say 'A Dancer', 'An Artist', instead of adding 'someone that was persecuted and hunted for daring to be'? Sometimes death feels like a sanitiser, Verna! Like a damn sanitiser! As if only in death are we allowed to be celebrated for the very deviance that made our time on this earth so damn gruelling. They will say I died of old age, and I will say 'No!', Verna. Put it on my plaque that I died a slow and drawn-out death, one that only the constraints of sexuality can bring. Put that on my damn plaque! Put a list of my achievements, a list of my credits, a list of my skills, and put in large writing the word DESPITE, or rather IN SPITE. That they cannot list what I did without mentioning it was DESPITE them. God, I hope whenever they hang me up on the wall, that we have got to a point where we live without the DESPITE. I wonder what we could be…. Oh Verna, scrap that last bit. Just have it end in despite.

Maud goes over to kiss Verna.

Maud: Verna, am I in love with you because you are the best secretary to ever live? Or are you the best secretary to ever live because I am in love with you?

A monologue for the part of Henry Cyril Paget, the 5th Marquess of Anglesey. The scene is somewhere beyond the notions of hours and years, in the way that only true iconic behaviour can bend time, yet, if you need a date: try the early 1900s. Paget is in his walk-in wardrobe, parading up and down as bailiffs come behind him to repossess his effects.

Paget: Was it worth it? Was it worth it, you ask? As you take my jewels, my dresses, my gowns, every shoe and heel I have spent my last penny on. You ask me: is it worth it? Is it worth it as you remove the crown on top of my crown, turn every hand-sewn diamond into a mere repossession? You ask me if it was worth it? Darling, I would grab the clock from your wall, turn back the hand and do it all over again. In a heartbeat. Just to experience the joy of defying you. I feel fuelled by your gossip. I wear 'Black Sheep' like a crest on my soon-to-be-unstitched gown. Was it worth it? Was it worth it, you ask? I wonder if a bird would choose never to fly and to die of old age, or to fly across continents knowing they will eventually be shot. Darling, I'd rather fly. To be limited by you and your rules is to be caged. Darling, take everything I own. For when I die poor and you are still gossiping, the coroner will see a smile on my face, a smile only possible when you have truly dared to be.

A PARTICIPATORY PIECE FOR THE UNEXPECTED SPECTATOR

(see p.45)

There comes a time in every show where audience participation is dreaded yet still happens.

This show is no different. For this scene is here to ensure the audience do not get too relaxed in their seats. To make sure they are not only comfortable with spectating. So often gender feels like something we gaze out on in others, let them do the heavy lifting of transgression, without ever turning the eyes inwards to watch how we transgress, or conform, or uphold, or dismantle. It is easy to look at SELF PORTRAIT IN A WEDDING DRESS and speak of all the ways Ajamu transgresses in the stillness of an image, but for how long has the Black queer subject done the work of all your revolutions. We let Ajamu continue to defy and stay lazy. That is not this play. For that. You must find A SELF PORTRAIT IN A WEDDING DRESS and look at it. Stare at the work for an uncomfortable amount of time, and then stare at it again. Stare at it some more. To then stare at yourself. And then you are ready to do this scene.

This text should be spoken in a whisper. The stage manager will bring you a mirror to hold up to

*yourself for this scene. Where there is a _____________,
speak out loud your own response, do not be
constrained by length. You can think about what you
might say, that is what rehearsals are for.*

You: The world expects me to be
_____________________ about my gender.

Stare at SELF PORTRAIT IN A WEDDING DRESS.

You: The first time I was corrected for displaying
gender wrong was _________________

Stare at yourself.

You: There was this one time, where I felt the weight
of expectations, it was ______________

Stare at SELF PORTRAIT IN A WEDDING DRESS.

You: The way I defy expectations is

____

*You hold up a mirror to yourself and say the next
text as you do....*

You: We can immortalise our defiance in this moment. Every day when we interact with the world, we hand over the camera and let others tell us where to stand, how to hold our shoulders, and what our photograph should look like. But our gender is not theirs to capture. We deserve autonomy. What they project onto it is their loss.

AN EPILOGUE BETWEEN OBJECTS

The curtains are closing. The gallery lights on stage are turning off. All the men and women – and those we could not define – are hanging up their portraits, packing away their sculptures: the angel of Jacob Epstein, the phalluses of Ithell Colquhoun's Scylla, *the* Mother and Child *of Barbara Hepworth. All that remains are Henry Moore's figures and their undulating forms. Centre stage. Ready to close out the show.*

Reclining Figure by Henry Moore (see p.46): It's good to finally relax. Who knew all you needed was to remove the trappings of flesh to feel free from gender.

Recumbent Figure by Henry Moore (see p.47): Someone tried to put a sticker on me today.

Reclining Figure: A sticker?! That's outrageous. You can't do that here.

Recumbent Figure: I didn't mind too much, because of what was on it. It said: 'It's ok to be trans.' I'd never felt so seen.

Reclining Figure: Maybe the feeling was mutual?

Recumbent Figure: What do you mean?

Reclining Figure: Out of all the faces, portraits, kings and queens, images of humans in flesh and robes and all the other places the kid could have put that sticker – they picked you. Maybe you are the one place they felt the most at home? As if in order to find something outside structures, we have to go outside of the body.

Recumbent Figure: I wouldn't survive around all those portraits.

Reclining Figure: How come?

Recumbent Figure: There is something that happens when you sit among other objects. Things that maybe once were inspired by a man's chest, or a woman's leg, or a mother's breast – things which have gone through so many shifts and changes that they are like a faint memory in the artist's mind. Like a stain that will always be there, but isn't the first thing you see. How nice is it for gender not to be the first thing we see among us.

Reclining Figure: I'm sure they still see it.

Recumbent Figure: Sure, if they look hard enough. But they can see something else first.

Or feel something. Or get somewhere else. It isn't holding us hostage. Maybe that is what all those before have aimed to do, to not be held hostage by gender…

The two Henry Moores raise what maybe looks like hands, as they raise a toast with what maybe looks like wine. As the curtains close behind them, and only the objects remain. Refusing to take a bow. Just staying still. Not wanting to partake in the performance of it all.

"SOME WORKS MAY NEVER HAVE ASKED FOR SUCH A LENS TO BE TURNED UPON THEM, BUT EQUALLY MANY OF US ASK NOT TO BE GENDERED, AND YET HERE WE ARE, GENDERED, WITHOUT A CHOICE, EVERY DAY. GENDER IS LIKE A FOG THAT CANNOT LIFT, OR A FILTER THAT CANNOT BE REMOVED, EVEN IN OUR CHOICE TO IGNORE IT – IT WILL STILL BE THERE."

"I BELIEVE ART IS ALSO WRAPPED UP IN PERFORMANCE. I SEE A PIECE OF ART AS A STILL OF A PERFORMANCE IN MOTION, A MOMENT OF DRAMA, A SNAPSHOT, A GLIMPSE INTO A SPECTACLE – IT CAPTURES A BREATH TO BE IMMORTALISED."

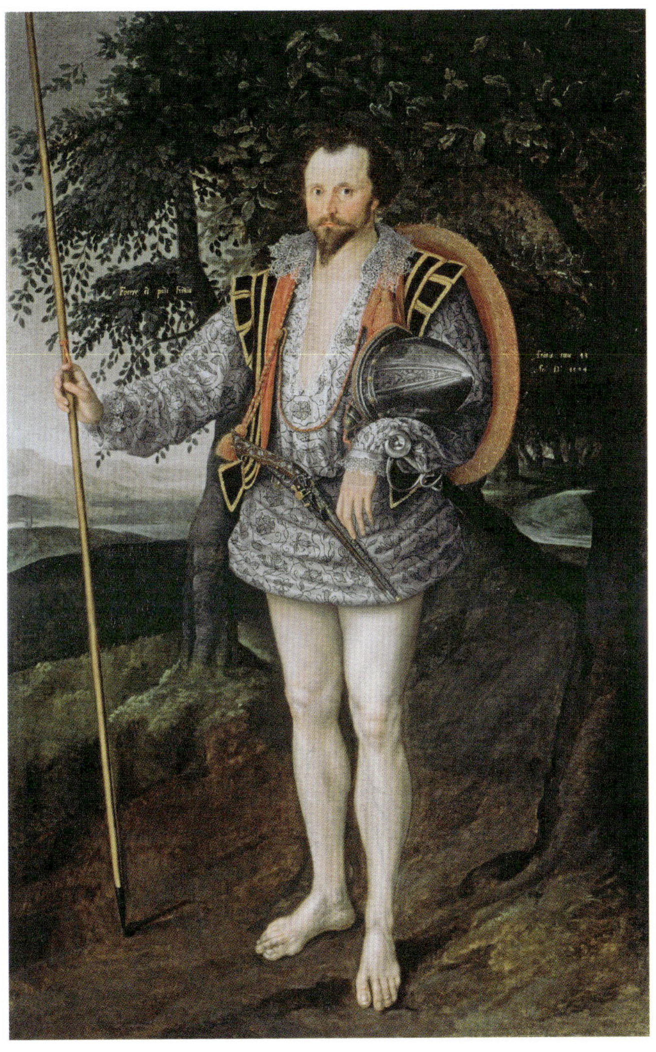

Marcus Gheeraerts II, *Portrait of Captain Thomas Lee* 1594, oil paint on canvas, 230.5 × 150.8, Tate

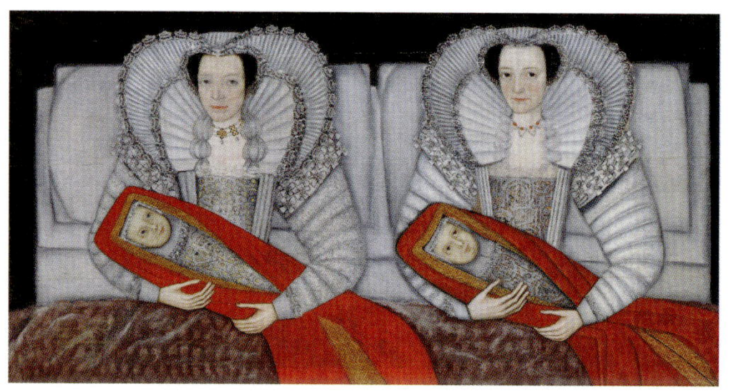

Unknown, *The Cholmondeley Ladies* c.1600–10, oil paint on wood,
88.6 × 172.3, Tate

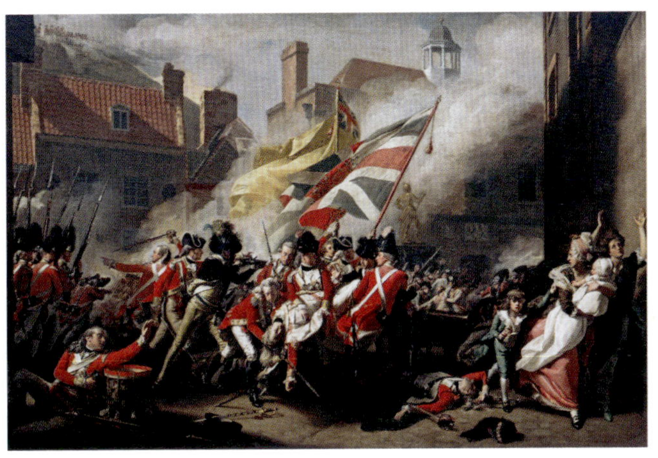

John Singleton Copley, *The Death of Major Peirso, 6 January 1781* 1783, oil paint on canvas, 251.5 × 365.8, Tate

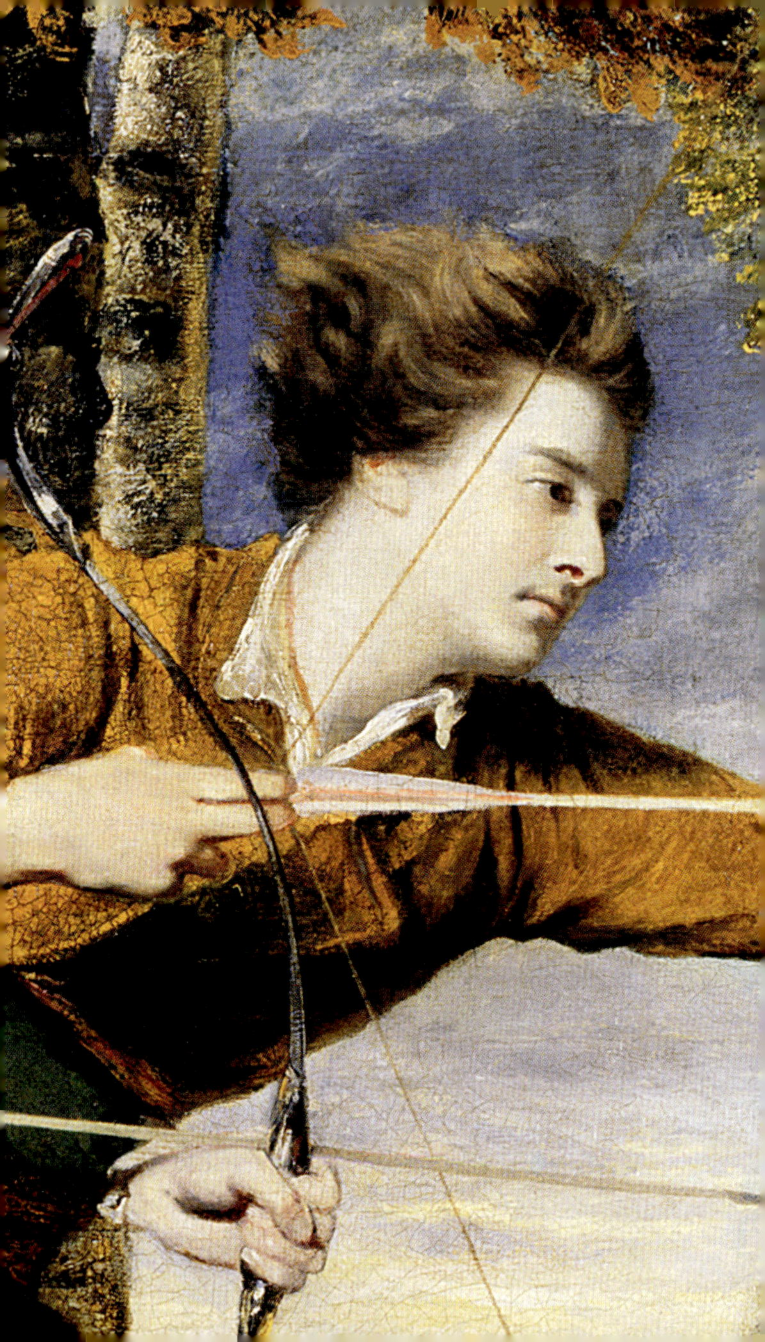

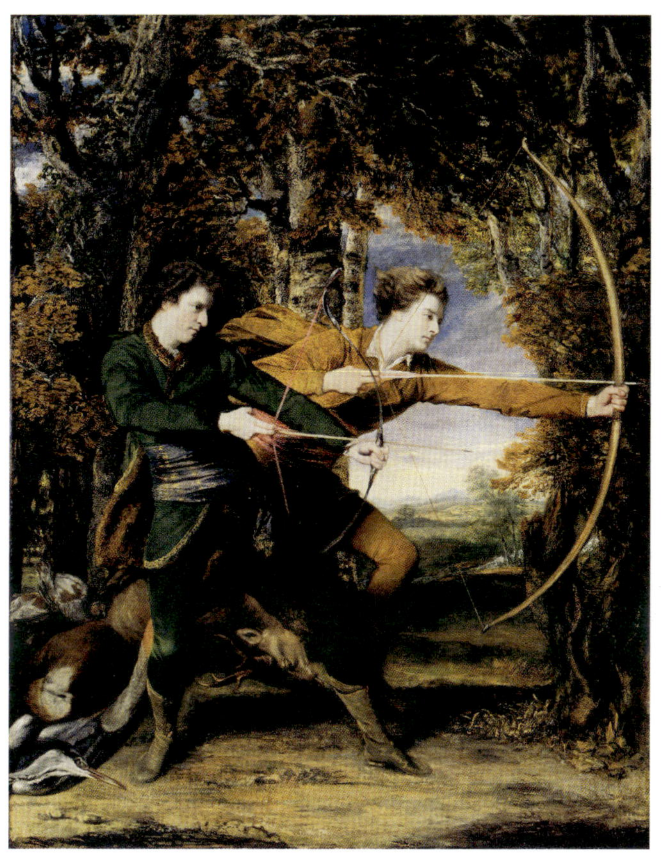

Sir Joshua Reynolds, *Colonel Acland and Lord Sydney: The Archers*
1769, oil paint on canvas, 236 × 180, Tate

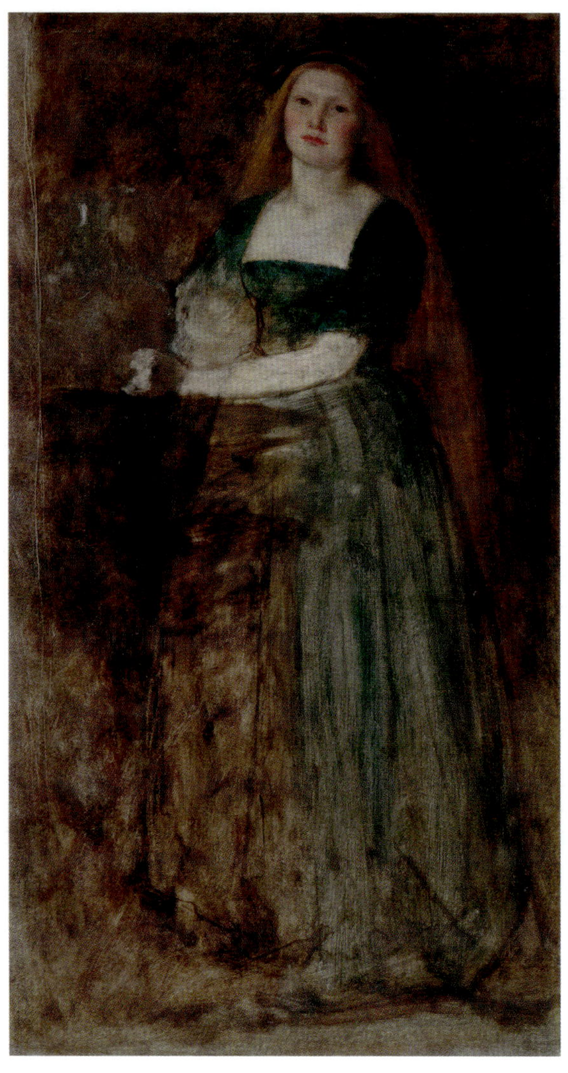

Joanna Mary Wells, *Gretchen* 1861, oil paint on canvas, 73 × 43.7, Tate

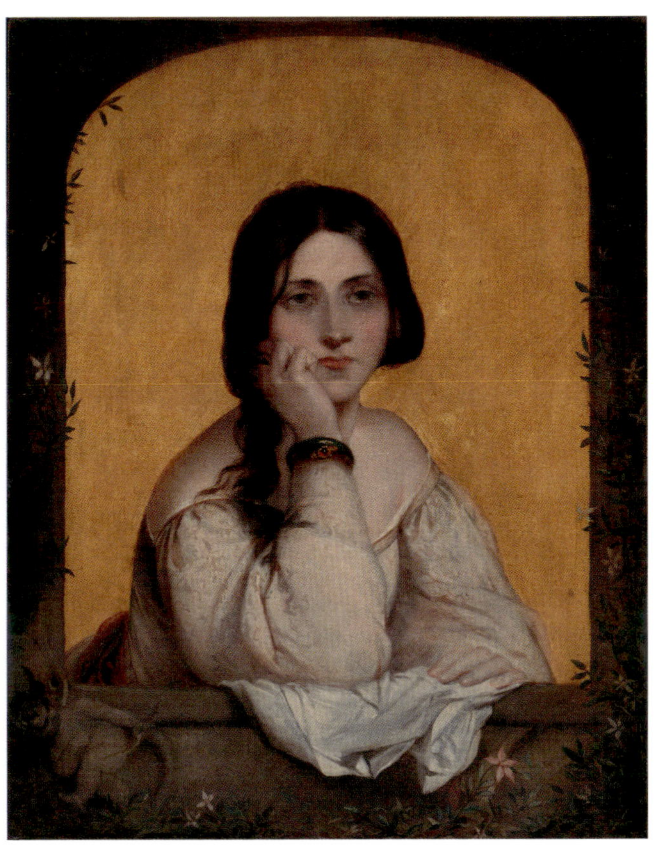

Theodore von Holst, *The Bride* 1842, oil paint on canvas, 92.3 × 71.3, Tate

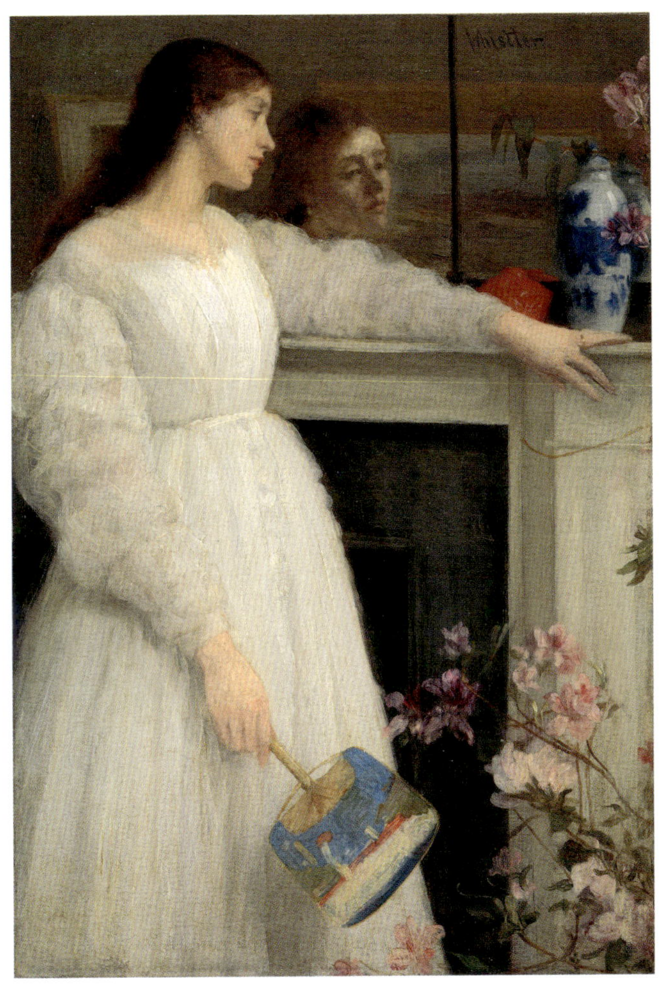

James Abbott McNeill Whistler, *Symphony in White, No.2: The Little White Girl* 1864, oil paint on canvas, 76.5 × 51.1, Tate

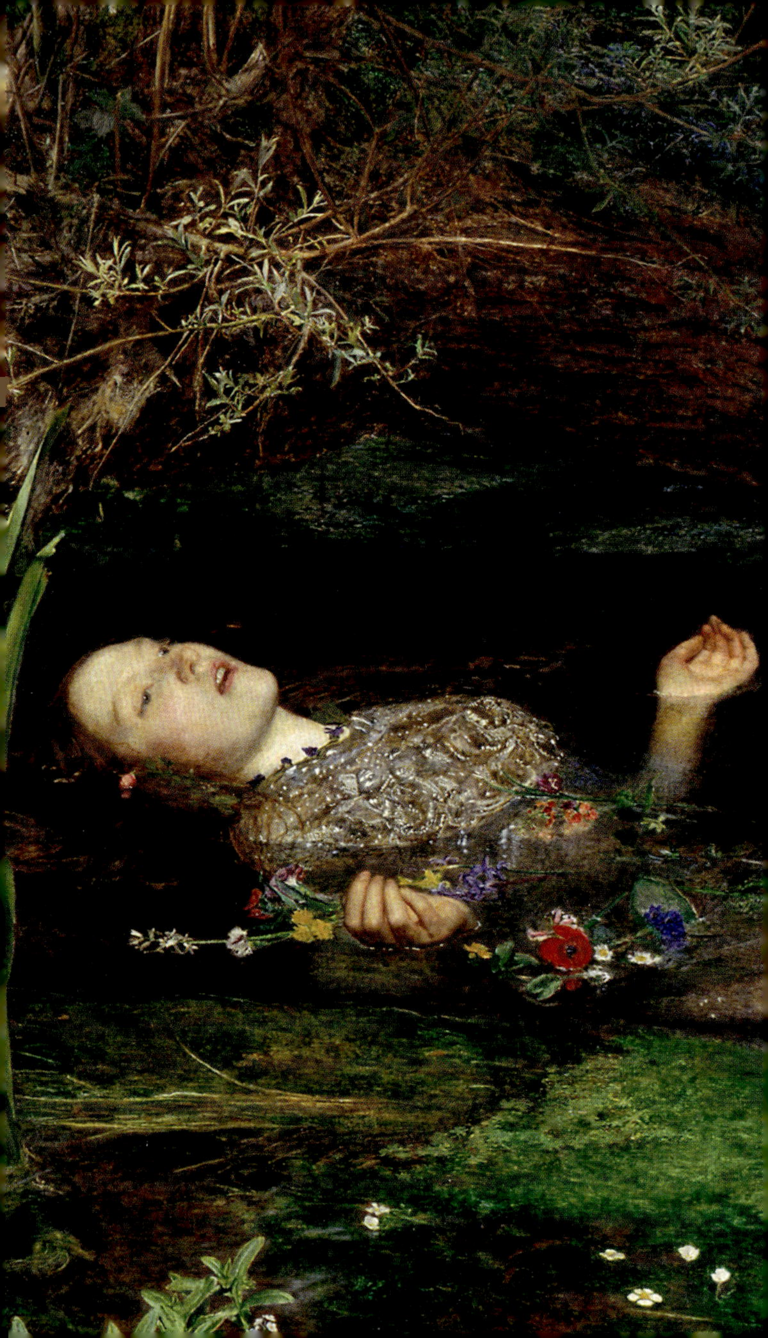

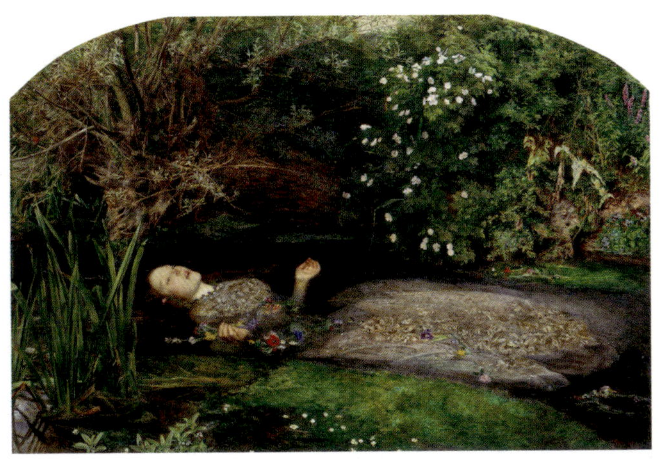

John Millais, *Ophelia* 1851–2, oil paint on canvas, 76.2 × 111.8, Tate

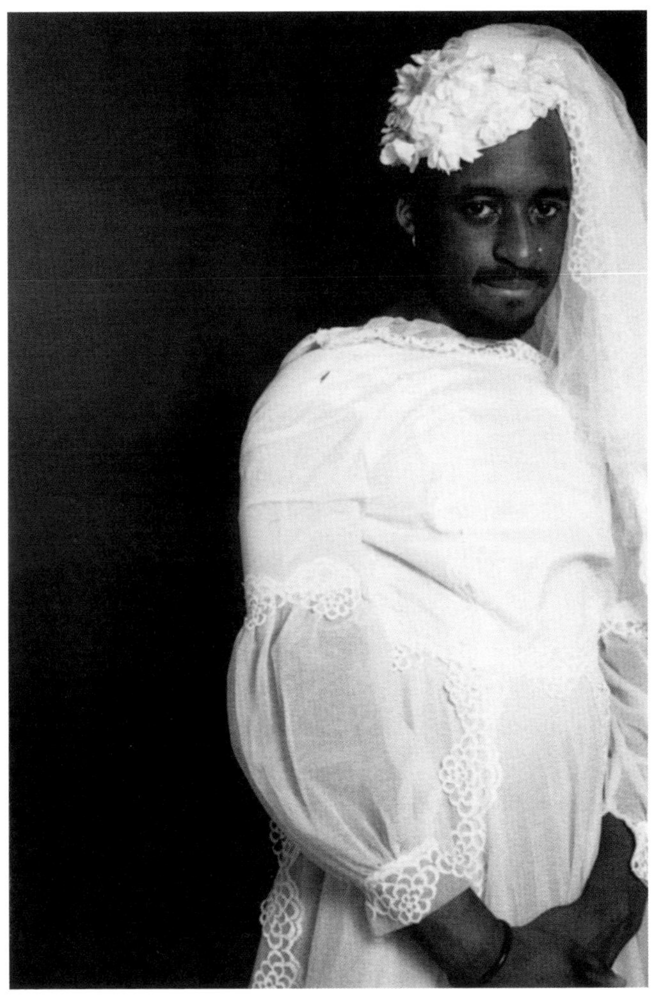

Ajamu, *Self-Portrait in Wedding Dress* 1993, photograph, gelatin silver print on paper, 7.7 x 5.1, Tate

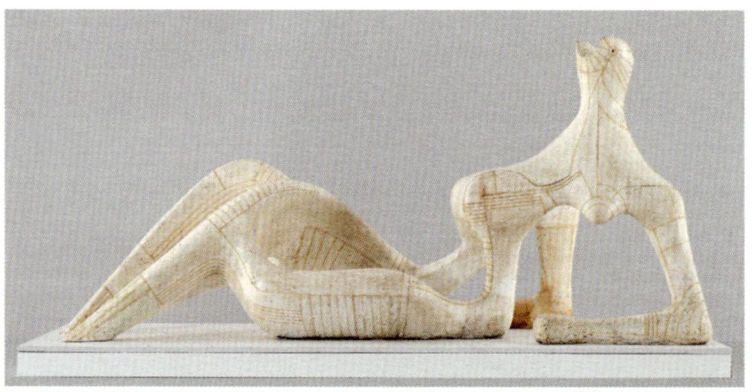

Henry Moore, *Reclining Figure* 1951, plaster and string,
105.4 × 227.3 × 89.2, Tate

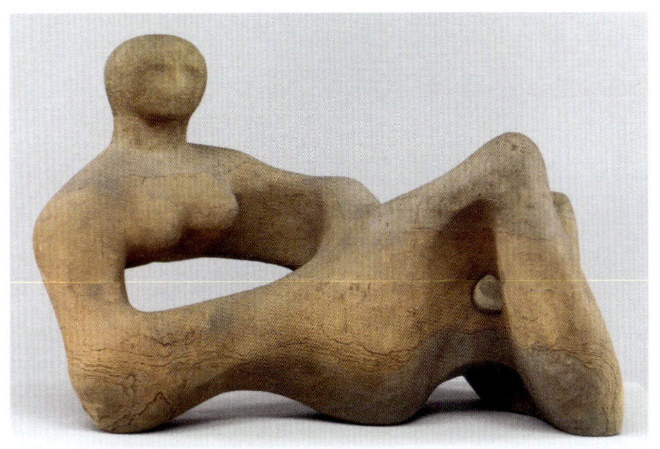

Henry Moore, *Recumbent Figure* 1938, green Hornton stone, 88.9 × 132.7 × 73.7, Tate